SPECIAL ★ OPS ★
Army Rangers
in Action

by Michael Sandler

Consultant: Fred Pushies
U.S. SOF Adviser

BEARPORT
PUBLISHING

New York, New York

Credits

Cover and Title Page, © Russ Bryant/Viper Images, Inc.; 4, © REUTERS/Sara K. Schwittek; 5, © U.S. Air Force photo by Senior Master Sgt. Rose Reynolds; 6, © Mitch Frazier/U.S. Army/Getty Images; 7, © G. Marc Benavidez/krtphotos/newscom.com; 8, © Three Lions/ Getty Images; 9, © Hulton-Deutsch Collection/CORBIS; 10, © Owen Franken/CORBIS; 11, © AP Images; 12, © National Archives; 13, © National Archives; 14, © Tech. Sgt. Ken Hammond; 15T, © Barry Williams/Getty Images; 15B, © Courtesy of Lynda Churilla on behalf of Peter Sprenger; 16, © Fred Pushies; 17, © Andrew Lichtenstein/Getty Images; 18, © Mansell/Time & Life Pictures/Getty Images; 19, © Bettmann/CORBIS; 20, © Bettmann/ CORBIS; 21, © Carl Mydans/Time Life Pictures/Getty Images; 22, © Hans Halberstadt dba Military Stock Photography; 23, © AP Images/Brennan Linsley; 24, © AP Images/Dave Martin; 25, © REUTERS/Dave Martin; 26, © Russ Bryant/Viper Images, Inc.; 27, © George Tiedemann/GT Images/Corbis; 28TL, © Kenn Mann; 28TR, © SSgt Fuqua, USAF; 28M, © Leif Skoogfors/CORBIS; 28B, © Courtesy of Blackhawk. 29T, © U.S. Army Photo by Staff Sgt. Bronco Suzuki; 29M, © Courtesy of U.S. Army; 29B, © REUTERS/Philippines.

Publisher: Kenn Goin
Senior Editor: Lisa Wiseman
Creative Director: Spencer Brinker
Design: Debrah Kaiser
Photo Researcher: Jennifer Bright

Library of Congress Cataloging-in-Publication Data

Sandler, Michael, 1965–
 Army Rangers in action / by Michael Sandler ; consultant Fred Pushies.
  p. cm. (Special ops)
 Includes bibliographical references and index.
 ISBN-13: 978-1-59716-632-4 (library binding)
 ISBN-10: 1-59716-632-4 (library binding)
 1. United States. Army—Commando troops—Juvenile literature. I. Title.

UA34.R36S315 2008
356'.1670973—dc22

                              2007039955

For more information, write to Bearport Publishing Company, Inc., 101 Fifth Avenue, Suite 6R, New York, New York 10003. Printed in the United States of America in North Mankato, Minnesota.

032011
030311CGC

10 9 8 7

Contents

Terrorists

On September 11, 2001, **terrorists** attacked the United States. Thousands of people were killed. America had to fight back. It wouldn't be an easy job. The terrorist leaders were hiding thousands of miles (km) away in Afghanistan.

The World Trade Center towers exploded into flames after being hit by two airplanes.

The World Trade Center in New York City and the Pentagon in Virginia were two of the terrorists' targets.

The U.S. government decided to quickly take action. Their first step was to **raid** an Afghan **airstrip** so that U.S. soldiers could use it to fight the terrorists. Who could do the job? The government called in a special group of soldiers—the Army Rangers.

Two hundred Rangers climbed into four planes. They headed to Afghanistan.

An MC-130 plane, such as this one, took the Army Rangers to Afghanistan.

U.S. Army Rangers

The Rangers are a special group of soldiers who handle the army's toughest **missions**. These jobs are called **special operations**, or special ops for short.

Rangers work anywhere—deserts, mountains, rivers, and swamps.

Rangers take over airports in others countries so that the enemy can't get away. They raid enemy camps to find and destroy weapons. They make surprise attacks on enemy soldiers before they can hurt U.S. troops.

Their missions are usually kept secret. Often the soldiers work at night when no one can see them. They travel quickly and quietly.

The Rangers are based at Fort Benning in Georgia.

Rangers are always ready to work. They can be anyplace in the world in just 18 hours!

The Ranger Way

The Rangers got their start in the 1600s with help from the Native Americans. During that time, most battles were fought in daylight. **Colonial soldiers** moved slowly in large groups toward the enemy.

Rogers' Rangers, led by Captain Robert Rogers, were American soldiers who fought with the British during colonial times.

Native Americans, however, fought differently. They moved at night and traveled in small groups. They taught the colonial soldiers to fight this way, too. Soon, people began to call the soldiers by a new name—Rangers. The Rangers way of fighting was so successful that during World War II (1939–1945), six Ranger **battalions** were formed.

Army Rangers running through fire as part of a training drill in 1943

In World War II, the United States, Britain, and other countries fought against Germany and Japan.

World War II: D-Day

One of the most important missions for the Rangers happened on **D-Day** during World War II. On June 6, 1944, **Allied soldiers** planned to land on the French coast, at a place called Pointe du Hoc. There, they would fight a battle to push the German army out of France.

Pointe du Hoc has 100-foot-high (30-m) cliffs.

They knew the battle would be fierce because the Germans had many cannons that were pointed toward the sea. The Rangers were given the job of destroying these guns before the Allied troops landed.

German soldiers loading a cannon

More than one million soldiers took part in the D-Day invasion.

Pointe du Hoc

Jack Kuhn and Leonard Lomell were two of the Army Rangers who helped with this mission. After their boat landed at Point du Hoc, they jumped onto the beach and ran toward the cliffs. They needed to get to the cannons that were kept on top of the cliffs.

Using rope and ladders, they tried to climb up the cliffs. However, it wasn't easy. The ropes were slippery and they had to avoid **grenades** being thrown at them by the German soldiers.

The Rangers used ladders to climb up the cliffs.

Somehow many Rangers, including Jack and Leonard, made it all the way up. Together they overpowered the Germans.

Then Jack and Leonard found the cannons and blew them up. Thanks to the Rangers, the cannons would never be used to hurt Allied soldiers.

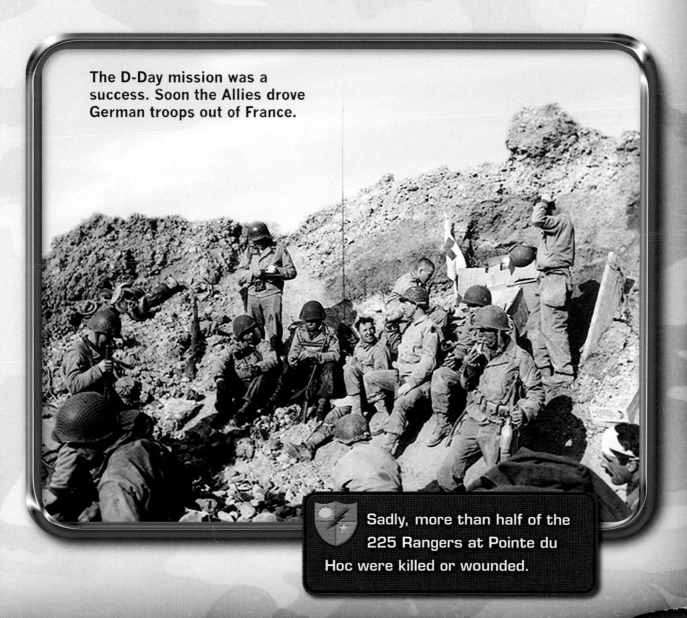

The **D-Day** mission was a success. Soon the Allies drove German troops out of France.

Sadly, more than half of the 225 Rangers at Pointe du Hoc were killed or wounded.

Army Ranger School

Becoming an Army Ranger is not easy work. Just ask Peter Sprenger. As part of his training, he had just done more push-ups than he could count. His legs ached from running for miles (km). Still, there was no time to rest. It was just another day in "crawl," the first part of Army Ranger School.

Army Ranger training begins with a test. Soldiers have to do 49 push-ups, 59 sit-ups, and run 5 miles (8 km) in 40 minutes.

The **obstacle course** was next. Peter would climb ladders and nets, and crawl through mud and under **barbed wire**. For the next two months, Peter and other soldiers would learn all the skills needed to be Rangers.

Soldiers crawling under barbed wire

During Ranger School, soldiers train almost 20 hours a day. This means they get only 4 hours of sleep.

Corporal Peter Sprenger

More Training

Once Peter finished the "crawl," he moved on to the second part of training called the "walk." This training takes place in the mountains. Peter learned climbing skills. He went on **patrols** in harsh, rugged conditions.

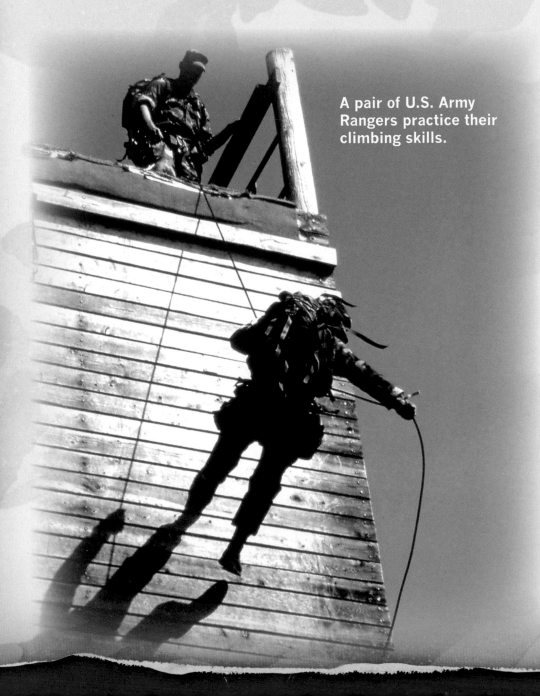

A pair of U.S. Army Rangers practice their climbing skills.

The final part of Ranger School is called the "run." Deep in a swamp, the trainees use all their **combat** skills. Peter practiced raids and other types of missions there.

Finally, Peter made it through training. He could crawl, walk, and run. He was ready to be an Army Ranger!

Only one out of four students makes it through all three parts of Ranger School.

Ranger School is so tough that most soldiers lose weight—20 pounds (9 kg) or more—by the end of training.

Japanese Prison Camps

Rescuing **prisoners of war** (POWs) is one type of mission Rangers train for. A very famous POW rescue took place during World War II.

Japanese soldiers leading **POWs** to a prison in the Philippines

During the war, many U.S. soldiers were captured by the Japanese. Some were held in terrible camps in the Philippines. Most prisoners were sick or starving. Many died each day. A Ranger rescue was their only hope. In January 1945, **commanders** Henry Mucci and Robert Prince set out for one of the camps with more than 100 Rangers.

Captain Robert Prince (left) and Lieutenant Colonel Henry Mucci (right) were two of the Army Rangers who led the raid on Camp Cabanatuan.

The Philippines is an island country in the Pacific Ocean. Japan took it over during World War II.

Rangers to the Rescue

The Rangers walked for miles (km) sneaking past Japanese soldiers and tanks. Finally, they reached the camp and crawled up to its fence.

The 6th Ranger Battalion raided Camp Cabanatuan in the Philippines in January 1945.

The **Filipinos** helped the Rangers in many ways. Some gave information about the Japanese camp. Others fought Japanese troops that tried to stop the rescue.

On signal, an American plane flew by to **distract** the Japanese guards. At that moment, the Rangers fired their guns and burst inside the camp. They found all the POWs. They led them outside, carrying those too sick to walk.

Nearby, Filipino villagers waited with carts. The Rangers loaded the prisoners onto the carts and took them away to a safe place.

More than 500 prisoners were rescued from Camp Cabanatuan.

Afghan Airstrip

Since World War II, Rangers have served in every U.S. war. In 2001, they led the first **commando** raid in Afghanistan. Being first was fine with the Rangers. After all, their **motto** is *Rangers Lead the Way*.

The mission's target was a **Taliban** airstrip. The Taliban was protecting the terrorists who were responsible for planning the September 11 attacks.

For years, all Rangers wore black berets. However, in 2001, they began wearing tan berets.

As their high-flying planes sped toward the airstrip, the Rangers were busy inside. They checked their equipment and reviewed the details of the mission.

Afghanistan is a country filled with mountains as well as deserts.

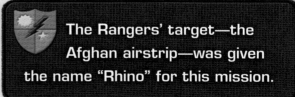

The Rangers' target—the Afghan airstrip—was given the name "Rhino" for this mission.

Mission Accomplished

After hours of flying, the planes arrived over Airstrip Rhino. The airplane doors opened. Rangers jumped out into the pitch-black night. They dropped through the darkness using **parachutes**. Hitting the ground, they quickly overtook the Taliban guards.

Airstrip Rhino

Then the Rangers spread out to the nearby buildings. They looked for traps and weapons.

The job took only a few hours. By sunrise, the airstrip was safe and ready for use by American soldiers. It was a mission well done for the Rangers!

One month later, Airstrip Rhino became Camp Rhino. It was an important base for American soldiers fighting in Afghanistan.

Camp Rhino was home to more than 1,000 Marines and sailors.

Rangers Lead the Way

No one looks forward to war. When war breaks out, however, a country wants its best soldiers fighting. Some of America's very best are the Army Rangers.

An Army Ranger prepared for a mission

The average Army Ranger is 24 years old, 5'9" (1.75 m), and has served in the military for $4\frac{1}{2}$ years.

Ranger missions are always changing. Today's Ranger **tactics** aren't the same as the ones used in World War II. One thing, though, will never change—when the United States goes to war, Army Rangers will lead the way.

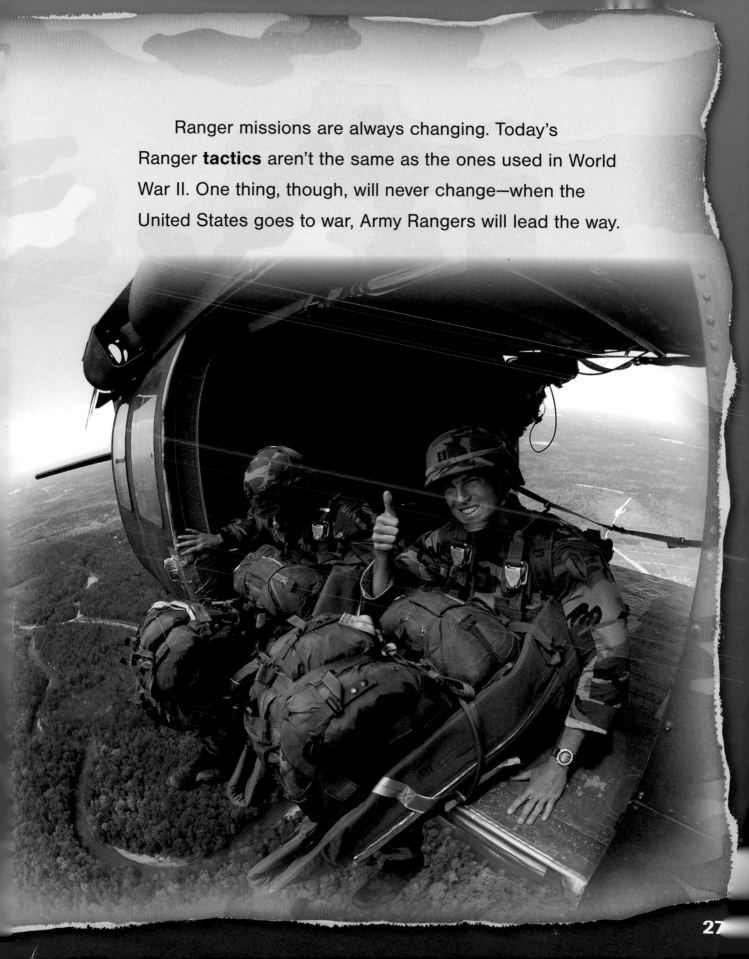

The Army Rangers' Gear

Army Rangers use lots of equipment to carry out their missions. Here is some of the gear they use.

Parachutes help the Rangers get to places that are hard to reach.

These **goggles** protect the Rangers' eyes from sun, wind, and dust.

The **Ranger Assault Carrying Kit** holds everything Rangers need: a radio, bullets, water bottles, maps, and tools.

Night Vision Goggles let Rangers see in the dark.

Body Armor protects Rangers from enemy fire.

The **M4 Carbine rifle** is easy to carry.

Glossary

airstrip (AIR-strip) a flat patch of ground used as a place to land planes on

Allied soldiers (AL-ide SOLE-jurz) the soldiers fighting for the group of countries that were battling Germany and Japan in World War II

barbed wire (BARBD WIRE) wire with small, sharp points along it, used for fences

battalions (buh-TAL-yunz) large groups of soldiers

colonial soldiers (kuh-LOH-nee-uhl SOLE-jurz) soldiers during the time when America was a British colony

combat (KOM-bat) fighting

commanders (kuh-MAND-erz) leaders of a group of soldiers

commando (kuh-MAN-doh) a sudden, quick raid

D-Day (DEE-day) June 6, 1944; the day when Allied forces invaded France during World War II

distract (diss-TRAKT) to keep from paying attention to something

Filipinos (*fil*-uh-PEE-nohz) people who are from the Philippines

grenades (gruh-NAYDS) small bombs that are thrown by hand

missions (MISH-uhnz) special jobs

motto (MOT-oh) a saying that states what someone believes in

obstacle course (OB-stuh-kuhl KORSS) a training course that is filled with hurdles, fences, and walls that soldiers must get over

parachutes (PAH-ruh-*shoots*) soft cloth devices used to slow one's fall after jumping out of a plane or helicopter

patrols (puh-TROHLZ) walks done by soldiers to make sure an area stays safe

prisoners of war (PRIZ-uhn-urz UHV WOR) soldiers who are captured and held by the enemy

raid (RAYD) to make a surprise attack

special operations (SPESH-uhl *op*-uh-RAY-shuhns) secret missions made by highly skilled groups of soldiers

tactics (TAK-tiks) ways of doing things to win a battle

Taliban (TAL-uh-*ban*) a military and political terrorist group that ruled Afghanistan from 1996 to 2001

terrorists (TER-ur-ists) groups that use violence and terror to get what they want

Bibliography

Bahmanyar, Mir. *Shadow Warriors: A History of the US Army Rangers*. Botley, Oxford: Osprey Publishing (2005).

Bryant, Russ and Susan. *75th Rangers*. St. Paul, MN: Zenith Press (2005).

Cavallaro, Gina. "Rakkasan Ranger." ArmyTimes.com, Vol. 66, Issue 5 (August 22, 2005).

Sides, Hampton. "Ghost Soldiers." *Esquire*, Vol. 135, Issue 5 (May, 2001).

Read More

Braulick, Carrie A. *The U.S. Army Rangers*. Mankato, MN: Capstone Press (2005).

Green, Michael, and Gladys Green. *The U.S. Army Rangers at War*. Mankato, MN: Capstone Press (2003).

Learn More Online

To learn more about the Army Rangers, visit
www.bearportpublishing.com/SpecialOps

Index

About the Author

Michael Sandler has written many books for children and young adults. He lives in Brooklyn, New York, with fellow writer Sunita Apte and their two children, Laszlo and Asha.